Aikido for Kids

Aikido
for Kids

by Laura Santoro
& Jennifer Corso

Photographs by Gerald F. Penca

Sterling Publishing Co., Inc.
New York

Acknowledgments

Domo (thanks!) to our Aikido models: *Students*: Shari-Danielle Easter, Brandon Parker, Jonah Petrinovic, C.J. Robinson, Nathan and Caroline Smith, Emily Stitz, and Kyra Walton; and *Parents and other models*: Dennis Anderson, J.S. Bonner, Luke Easter, Irene Gaspar, Kim Murley and, of course, each other—Laura and Jennifer.

A special "thank you" to Kim Murley for her assistance; to Gerald and Robin Penca for their skill and knowledge; to Sheila Anne Barry, our editor Claire Bazinet and everyone at Sterling Publishing; to our families and friends for their support; and to all our teachers and fellow Aikido students.

Library of Congress Cataloging-in-Publication Data
Santoro, Laura.
    Aikido for kids / by Laura Santoro & Jennifer Corso;
photographs by Gerald F. Penca.
      p.   cm.
    Includes index.
    Summary: An introduction to the martial art of aikido which
comes from Japan and which demonstrates how one's spirit can
be brought into harmony with the world.
    ISBN 0-8069-9405-3
    1. Aikido—Juvenile literature. 2. Martial arts for children—Juvenile
literature. [1. Aikido. 2. Martial arts.] I. Corso, Jennifer. II. Penca,
Gerald F., ill. III. Title.
GV1114.35.S24   1998
796.815'4—dc21   98-44563
                                         CIP
                                         AC

10 9 8 7 6 5 4 3 2 1

Published by Sterling Publishing Company, Inc.
387 Park Avenue South, New York, N.Y. 10016
© 1998 by Laura Santoro and Jennifer Corso
Distributed in Canada by Sterling Publishing
℅Canadian Manda Group, One Atlantic Avenue, Suite 105, Toronto,
Ontario, Canada M6K 3E7
Distributed in Great Britain and Europe by Chris Lloyd, 463 Ashley Road,
Parkstone, Poole, Dorset, BH14 0AX, England
Distributed in Australia by Capricorn Link (Australia) Pty Ltd.
P.O. Box 6651, Baulkham Hills, Business Centre, NSW 2153, Australia
Manufactured in the United States of America

Sterling ISBN 0-8069-9405-3

Contents

What Is Aikido?

What is Aikido? Aikido is a martial art that comes from Japan.

Each part of the word "aikido" has a meaning.

"Ai" means harmony...

..."ki" means spirit...

...and "do" means the way or path.

So, "Aikido" means the way of bringing your spirit into harmony with the world around you.

In Aikido, the teacher is called *sensei* ("sen-say").

The founder of Aikido is called *O Sensei*, which means "great teacher."

Aikido is practiced in a place called a *dojo* ("doe-joe"). Many dojos have a place on a wall that is called a *shomen* ("show-men"). This space is used to display pictures or things that remind us of the spirit of Aikido. You may see a picture of O Sensei, a Japanese drawing, or even flowers.

Aikido is about working *with* other people, not against them. Fighting against someone is hard—it takes energy.

Being friends with people is easier—you are working with each other. "Working with" is what Aikido is all about—combining your energy with someone else's energy.

Now you know a little about Aikido. This book will teach you even more.

You will learn how to bow...

...some warm-ups and stretches...

...and the
Aikido
stance.

You will find out how
to do breathing exercises...

...and knee-walking.

You will also learn how to fall...

...some Aikido grabs...

...and how to do Aikido movements with a partner.

This book will show you what happens during an Aikido test...

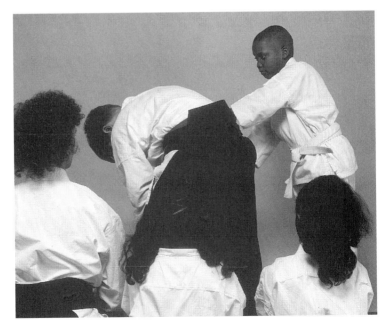

...and how your parents can help you find a good Aikido class.

In Aikido, you learn how to treat people with respect. People who respect each other do not need to get into fights. This is the best way to use what you learn in Aikido.

Remember, Aikido is a martial art. If you are practicing with a friend, treat him or her with respect. Be safe, and have fun!

Getting Started

When practicing Aikido, you should wear a white practice outfit called a *dogi* (pronounced "doe-ghee").

You will also wear a belt. The color of your belt shows your rank in the practice of Aikido. As a beginner, the first belt you will wear is white.

You may also wear a *hakama* (hah-kah-mah). A hakama is a pair of big, loose pants that looks almost like a skirt.

You should treat your dogi, belt and hakama with respect. A dogi should be kept neat and clean. A hakama requires special care, and must be folded carefully after each class. Your belt is a symbol of your rank and should also be cared for properly.

At the beginning and end of Aikido classes, and while listening to your sensei, you will sit in *seiza* ("say-zah").

Keep your back straight and your head up when you are in seiza position.

In Aikido, you will often bow from seiza. Bowing is a sign of respect. The bow from seiza is called a *formal bow*. To do a formal bow, place your hands on the floor in front of you and bend at the waist. You will do a formal bow when you begin to work with a partner.

You will also do a formal bow when you bow to your sensei.

You can also do a bow from a standing position.

Stand straight, with your feet together and your hands at your sides. Bend forward from your waist.

You do a standing bow when you enter or leave the *dojo* (the practice hall) and when you finish working with a partner.

■ Warm-Up Exercises

Before you do Aikido, or any other exercise, you should warm up and stretch. The more you warm up before exercising, the less likely you are to get hurt or become sore.

STRETCHES

There are many stretches you can do in Aikido. Here are a few for you to try.

Side Stretch

Stand with your feet placed as far apart as your shoulders (shoulder width). Raise your left arm above your head and take a deep breath. Let your breath out slowly and lean to the right as far as you can.

Always remember to be careful when you are exercising. If you feel any pain, stop what you are doing and either try again more slowly, or move on to something else. Do your stretching slowly and carefully. If you hurt yourself, you will not be able to practice Aikido.

Stand up straight again, and this time lift your right hand as you breathe in. Let your breath out and stretch to the left. Stretch to both sides two more times.

Arm Swing
Keep your feet shoulder
width apart. Twist your hips
to the left and swing your
arms back.

Now turn your hips to the
right and swing your arms
to the other side. Do this
five times on each side.

Neck Stretches

Tip your head forward and count slowly to five...then tip your head back and count to five again.

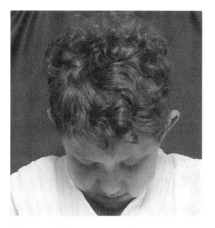 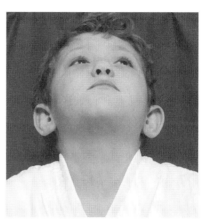

Repeat these stretches two more times.

Turn your head slowly to the right...then to the left.

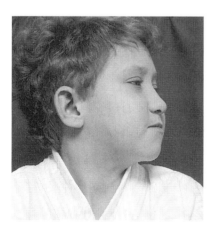 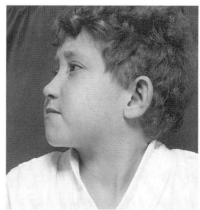

Do this two more times, also.

Wrist Stretch
Hold an arm out in front of
you with your palm facing up.
Reach out and place your other
hand across your fingers.

Push down on your fingers and
stretch your hand toward your knee.
Change hands. Do this stretch two
times for each hand.

Shake out your hands and wrists.

Side Leg Stretch

Spread your legs wide apart, with your toes pointing forward.
Bend your right knee, and lean to the right side, stretching
your left leg.

Come back to the center position, then bend your left knee and
lean to the left side. Make sure both feet stay flat on the floor!
Hold each stretch for ten seconds, and repeat on each side.

Seated Leg Stretch

Sit on the floor with your legs spread apart as far as they will go. Put your hands on the floor in front of you, and push them out as far as you can. Hold this stretch while you count to ten.

Remember, stretches should be done slowly, and should not hurt. Only stretch as far as you are able to do comfortably. If you do these stretches regularly, you will become more and more flexible.

Keep your knees straight and reach for your left foot. Hold this stretch while you count to ten.

Now see if you can touch the toes on your right foot.

Count to ten on this side, too.

Foot Stretch

Keep your legs straight and bring your feet together. Push the toes on your left foot forward as far as you can, while you pull your right foot back.

Now switch—push the toes on your right foot forward and pull your left foot back. Do this four more times on each side.

■ Meditation

For Aikido training, you need to warm up more than just your body. Your mind must be calm and clear. If you panic or become angry, you may lose your balance or forget what to do next.

Meditation is a way of preparing your mind. There are many ways to meditate. One easy way is to sit in seiza with your eyes closed and pay attention to your breathing. Breathe in through your nose and out through your mouth. Breathe slowly, until you are relaxed and very calm. Now you are ready for Aikido practice.

Aikido Basics

■ The Aikido Stance

There is only one main stance in Aikido, and it is called *hanmi* ("hahn-me"). To get into right hanmi, simply step forward from a standing position with your right foot.

In a right hanmi, the toes of your left foot should turn slightly outward, and the middle of your foot should be lined up behind your right heel.

To get into a left hanmi, you step forward with your left foot and line your right foot up behind your left.

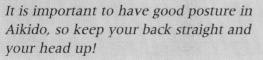

It is important to have good posture in Aikido, so keep your back straight and your head up!

In Aikido, you learn to move from the "center" of your body. Your center is an inch or two below your bellybutton, inside your body. If you learn to use your center, you will be using your whole body at the same time. Then, you will be able to use Aikido on almost anyone.

■ Developing Your Center

Now you will learn how to move from your center.

You will learn the rowing exercise...

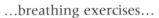

...breathing exercises...

...and knee-walking.

ROWING EXERCISE

One way to learn to move from your center is to do the *rowing exercise.* Start in hanmi, bend your knees, and bring your hands up to your waist. Bend your front knee. Breathe in as you push your hands out over your front foot.

Bring your hands back in as you bend your back knee. This will move your center back. Bend your back knee even more, and breathe out as you bring your hands near your hips. Breathe in again, bend your front knee, and push your hands out.

Repeat the exercise a few more times, then change hanmi and do it on the other side.

BREATHING EXERCISES

Another way to develop your center is to do breathing exercises. When you practice Aikido, your belly should move in and out with each breath.

Sit in seiza. Hold your hands, palm up, out in front of you.

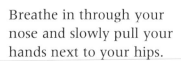

Breathe in through your nose and slowly pull your hands next to your hips.

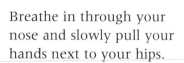

Hold your breath and turn your hands over.

Breathe out through your mouth and push your hands forward.

Do this twenty times, or until you feel calm and relaxed.

Here is another breathing exercise to do in seiza.

Bring your hands together in front of you.

Breathe in through your nose and lift your hands above your head.

Hold your breath and let your hands drop slowly to your sides.

Bring your hands beside your hips.

Breathe out as you push your hands out in front of you.

KNEE-WALKING

A good way to make your center stronger is to practice something called knee-walking.

You start knee-walking by sitting in seiza. Prop yourself up on your toes and sit back on your heels.

To knee-walk, lift your right knee and push it out in front of you by turning your hips.

Set your right knee down.

Now lift your left knee and push it in front of you with your hips.

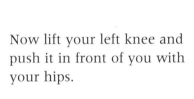

Set your left knee down. Repeat these movements, switching between your right knee and your left knee. Be sure to keep your feet together as you knee-walk.

■ Safe-Place Movements

One of the most important ideas in Aikido is to "get out of the way"! That means if someone is trying to attack you, you need to move your body to a safe place.

In Aikido, there are two basic movements you can do to get out of the way. The first is *irimi* ("ear-ee-me"), or "entering." Start in hanmi.

Slide your front foot forward.

Keeping your feet in place, pivot—so that you face backward from where you started.

Slide your front foot backwards until you are in hanmi.

There is another way to "get out of the way."

The second get-out-of-the-way move is *tenkan* ("ten-kan").
The word tenkan means "turning." To do tenkan, start in hanmi
with your arms in front of you—you can pretend that you are
holding a giant beach ball.

Keep your front foot in place and *spin backwards, making a* half-circle.

You should end up in hanmi again.

■ Falling

Aikido has many throws, so one of the most important things to learn is how to fall properly. These next pages show you how to do a backward fall...

...a forward roll from kneeling position...

...and a forward roll from standing.

Important! *Before you start practicing rolls, ask your parents to help you find a good place to try them. You should not start practicing rolls on a hard floor. You will need a soft spot, like a gymnastics mat or a very thick rug.*

BACKWARD FALL

To do an Aikido backward fall, first get into hanmi.

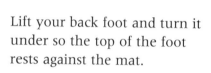

Lift your back foot and turn it under so the top of the foot rests against the mat.

Sink gently down onto your back knee until you are sitting on the floor.

Tuck your chin against your chest and roll onto your back.

Rock forward onto one leg, with the other knee off the ground.

Stand back up in hanmi without using your hands.

FORWARD ROLL

The forward rolls of Aikido are different from somersaults. In an Aikido roll, you use only one hand, and your head does not touch the ground.

Start your forward roll from a kneeling position. Place your hands palm down on the ground in front of you, and point your front elbow straight ahead.

Roll slowly up your front arm until your shoulder touches the ground.

Tuck your chin to your chest and roll from your front shoulder...

...to the opposite hip.

Come back up to a kneeling position.

You should not feel any part of your body thump against the ground when you roll. If you do, imagine you are a big, round ball and try again.

Do not give up if you feel you have not done the first few rolls just right. Everything in Aikido takes practice. Try a few more times and see if you get better. Practice your rolls on both sides.

STANDING ROLL

When you feel you can do kneeling rolls well, it is time to try standing rolls.

Start in a hanmi. Which of your feet is in front?

Place the hand on that side (right or left) on the ground next to your front foot. Once again, point your elbow forward.

Push off with your back leg and roll up your arm...

...and across your body, just as you did from the kneeling position.

Come back up into hanmi.

■ Strikes and Grabs

Aikido teaches you how to defend yourself from many different kinds of attacks. We will go over a few of the basic strikes and grabs here.

If you grab someone's right wrist with your left hand, or left wrist with your right hand, you are doing a *same-side grab*.

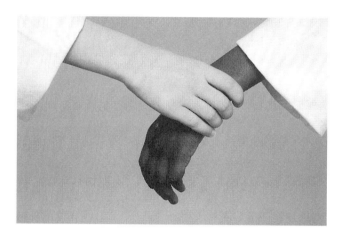

If you grab someone's right wrist with your right hand (almost as if you were shaking hands) or left wrist with your left hand, you are doing a *cross-hand grab*.

You can also grab both of your partner's wrists at the same time.

Now let's learn some strikes.

Stand in hanmi. To strike, begin to raise the hand that is on the same side as your back foot.

As one hand is raised over your head, the other hand is in front of you to protect yourself.

Step forward with your back foot while striking downwards with the edge of your lifted hand. Your hand should come down right on top of a partner's forehead. This strike is called a *shomenuchi* ("show-men-oo-chee").

Important: *When you are practicing with a partner, always stop a strike or a punch before contact. In Aikido, you are in control and do not actually hit.*

Now try another strike. Start in hanmi again.

Hold your front hand out to protect yourself and curl your rear hand into a fist. Your thumb should be on the outside of your fist.

As you step forward with your rear foot, pull back with your forward hand and punch out with your fist. Aim your strike at just below the ribs. This is a *munetsuki* ("moo-net-ski") strike. Notice that you do not actually allow the punch to hit your partner.

Putting It Together

Now you will be able to see how basic Aikido moves work when you have a partner.

You will learn how to move safely away from attacks...

...how to control your partner's center...

...use your breath to
make techniques work...

...and a game that will
teach you how to blend
with a partner.

■ Basic Escape Moves

You can use *tenkan* (turning) or *irimi* (entering), the two basic escape movements, to get away from any of the strikes or grabs you learned in the last chapter. Practice the strikes and movements in slow motion.

To start, you and your partner should both be in the same hanmi. Your partner makes a fist. Now, here's how to do the irimi from munetsuki.

As your partner begins to strike, slide your front foot forward. Pivot into irimi on the same side as your partner's punch.

Place your front hand on your partner's elbow, and your back hand on your partner's back shoulder. You are now in a safe place.

You can also use a tenkan to escape the same attack.

Start in the same side hanmi as your partner.

As your partner punches out, slide your front foot off to the side and do a tenkan. Place your hand on the wrist of your partner's punching hand—you are out of the way!

You can also do a tenkan to get out of the way if your partner strikes sho-menuchi, a strike at the top of your head.

When your partner raises his hand to strike, take a hanmi, with your front foot on the same side as the attacking hand.

Do a tenkan as your partner's hand comes down. You will end up safely beside him.

What if your partner grabs you instead? You can still do a tenkan or irimi.

Let's say your partner does a same-side wrist grab and pushes. If your partner grabs your left hand, get into left hanmi. If your partner grabs your right hand, move into right hanmi.

Slide your front foot beside your partner's foot and do a tenkan. You should end up behind your partner, where she cannot punch or kick you.

■ Control of the Center

The goal of Aikido is to be able to control your partner so that neither you nor your partner are hurt. You do this by controlling your partner's whole body, especially his center. If you only control your partner's arm or hand, he will have his other arm and his legs to punch and kick you. A simple way to learn how to affect your partner's center is to practice *kokyu* ("coke-yoo.")

Have your partner get into hanmi, grab your wrists and push. Get into the same hanmi, right or left, as your partner. Then take a deep breath.

As you breathe out, drop one shoulder and turn the other hand so that your palm faces your opponent.

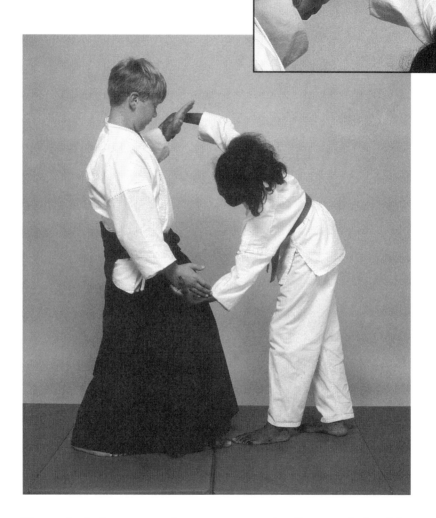

If you do kokyu correctly, your partner's elbow and shoulder will go up and her center will turn slightly.

Now you can do the heaven-and-earth throw. When you have done kokyu, slide your back foot forward and push your lower hand toward the floor.

Bend your knees and lead your partner into a back fall.

As you keep bending your knees, push your partner gently backwards. This is a good way for your partner to practice back falls.

You can practice kokyu with both hands in a special breathing exercise. Sit facing a partner. You should both be in seiza. Ask your partner to grab your wrists and push.

Take a deep breath. As you breathe out, drop your shoulders and raise both hands so that your palms face your partner.

Turn your left hand over and push down toward the floor. Turn your whole body, arms and all, to the left. Your partner will start to fall over.

Sit up on your toes and keep your arms round, as if you are holding a large beach ball right above your partner's nose. Now, see if your partner can push you over.

One of the most important ways of controlling your partner's center is *ikkyo* ("eek-yo"), which means "first technique." Let's try and ikkyo from a shomenuchi. In preparation, as your partner begins to raise his hand up to strike, get into a good hanmi, with your hands in front of you for protection. Your front foot should be on the same side as his striking hand.

As your partner continues to pull his hand up, place your front hand on his elbow, and your back hand on his wrist. Push your partner's elbow toward his ear.

This causes your partner to turn away from you.

Bend your knees and lower your partner to the floor.

Sink to your knees and guide your partner to the mat.

Do these movements slowly at first, and try to move your partner's whole body. If you are having trouble, do not do the movements faster and harder. Keep your mind calm, and practice until your movements feel easy and natural.

■ Breath Throws

Many throws in Aikido are called "breath throws." This is not because you breathe on your partner and he falls down, but because you use your breathing to give the throw extra power.

You can do a breath throw when faced with munetsuki. Remember that you should be in the same hanmi as your partner.

As your partner punches out, do an irimi. Place your hands on your partner's shoulders.

Step back with your front foot. Move your other foot beside your partner's back foot.

Pull gently back and down on your partner's shoulders. Your partner will get ready to take a back fall.

Breathe out as you bend your knees and push your hands down. Push slowly enough that your partner can take a proper fall.

Another breath throw can be done to escape from a two-hand grab. This throw will also give your partner a chance to practice his forward rolls.

First, make sure that you are in hanmi when your partner has hold of both your wrists.

When he pushes, bring your hands to your center and step back with your front foot.

Breathe out as your sink down on your back foot and push your hands to the outside of your back knee.

Help your partner take a forward roll by pushing your arms farther back.

The exact movement you do will be different each time you try an Aikido technique. This is because each partner is different—taller, shorter, stronger, weaker—and each attack is different—faster, slower, harder, softer.

If you need help figuring out exactly what to do in a certain movement, find a good Aikido teacher to help you.

Listen carefully to your sensei. He or she is there to help you. Remember that it takes years of practice to learn how to apply Aikido movements to many different situations.

▪ Learning to Blend

Through Aikido practice, you will learn to blend with your partner's strikes and grabs. You can do this by playing a special
blending game with a partner. It's called the "mirror game."

Sit in seiza
across from a
partner. Hold
your hands up
and have your
partner match
her hands to
yours.

Now move
your hands
around slowly.
Your partner
tries to match
your move-
ments exactly,
so that it
seems almost
as if you are
looking in a
mirror!

Switch after a while, so that your partner gets a chance to lead
and you try to follow. As you get better at blending, ask your
partner to move faster and see if you can keep up!

Testing

Most Aikido schools do not go to tournaments or hold contests. This is because Aikido is not about winning or losing. It is about cooperating with a partner and helping each other learn.

You show that you are getting better in Aikido by testing. During testing, you prove to your sensei, your fellow students, and yourself that you have learned new techniques and have gotten better at the techniques you already knew. You also earn rank by testing.

You test with a partner. To start the test, you and your partner do a seated bow to a picture of O Sensei.

Then, you bow
to your sensei...

...and to your
partner.

Next, your sensei will call out what she would like you to do.

Sometimes you will show a technique
with a partner...

...and sometimes you will show a
roll or fall by yourself.

When your test is over, you will bow again to O Sensei's picture, to your sensei and to your partner. Then you will wait and watch while other students take their test.

When everyone has finished, your sensei will make comments about what she saw during the test.

If you have passed your test, sensei will call you up before the class. She will congratulate you, and you may receive a new belt!

Then your sensei will honor *you* with a bow...

...and your classmates and other teachers will cheer!

Now, you can put on your new colored belt.

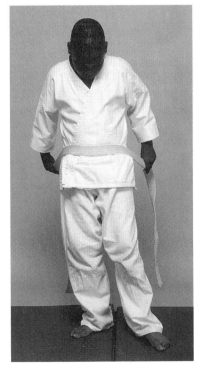

Remember that with a higher rank comes more responsibility. You will be expected to set a good example for newer students and help the sensei in the dojo.

Learning More
About Aikido

So now you have learned a little bit about Aikido in the dojo.

Think of other ways to use Aikido in your life. Recycling cans, bottles or newspaper is Aikido because you are living in harmony with nature by saving our natural resources.

Making friends is Aikido because you are blending your two spirits together.

Paying attention to your parents and your teachers is Aikido because you are showing respect for those who teach and protect you.

Thank you for reading our book about Aikido. If you want to learn more Aikido, talk to your parents about finding an Aikido class near you. Visit a dojo with your parents. Your parents can talk to the senseis there about classes.

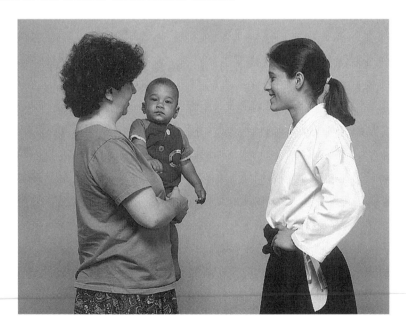

Don't be afraid to ask questions. Talk to the other students, too. Hopefully, you'll become part of an Aikido dojo!

Domo arigato gozaimashita – Thank you very much!

Glossary of Terms

center	balancing point of the body
dogi	white practice outfit; for short, also called a "gi"
dojo	practice hall
hakama	loose-legged pants
ikkyo	first technique
irimi	"getting out of the way" move; entering
hanmi	standing position, with one foot slightly forward of the other
kokyu	a breath move affecting an opponent's center
munetsuki	a strike with a fist, a punch
O Sensei	great teacher
seiza	sitting position, back on the heels
sensei	teacher
shomen	a shrine, usually on the dojo wall
shomenuchi	a downward strike with the edge of the hand
tenkan	another "getting out of the way" move; turning

A Word for Parents

In this book, we have tried to show children a little bit about Aikido—what it means to practice Aikido physically, and mentally, too. But this book can only teach them the basics. If your children like what they have learned here, we hope you will help them to learn more by finding an Aikido class near your home. Here are some tips that will help you find the right Aikido school for your child.

1 Always go to observe a class before enrolling your child. You should also take your son or daughter to observe a class. A good way to find out if your child is old enough for Aikido is if he or she can sit and watch a full class. If so, the child should be able to take that class.

2 Talk to the instructor (sensei), and ask questions. What are the age ranges for the class? How many children are in each class? How many teachers or other adult students are there? Be wary of schools that promise belts in set periods of time—you are paying for your child to learn Aikido, not just to have colored belts given to them regardless of skill.

3 Talk to other parents. Are the children treated equally and with respect? Do they have fun in class, but still learn?

4 Sign your child up for only a month or two, to start. A child has to enjoy Aikido and has to want to learn. You can tell in a short time whether your child really wants to go to class.

5   If you like what you see, consider joining an adults' class
yourself. Aikido can be a fun family activity when everyone
learns together. Some dojos even offer combined classes for
family members. (Just don't be discouraged if your children
learn how to roll faster than you do—kids roll naturally.)

We hope that you help your child foster his or her interest in
martial arts and Aikido, and we welcome your comments or any
questions that you may have about Aikido and children's classes.

Laura Santoro and Jennifer Corso

Index

About the Authors

LAURA SANTORO holds a black belt in Aikido under the instruction of Shihan Mitsugi Saotome of the Aikido Schools of Ueshiba (ASU). She has taught children's Aikido classes since 1991 and has been the chief instructor of children's Aikido programs since 1993. Laura also teaches adult Aikido classes. Her other martial arts endeavors include producing and hosting "Western Warrior," a weekly martial arts radio program for WRUW-FM, Cleveland, Ohio.

JENNIFER CORSO began training in Aikido in 1987. She has taught children's Aikido classes since 1992. Outside of the dojo, Jennifer practices labor law in Cleveland.

Co-authors Laura Santoro and Jennifer Corso live and practice Aikido in the greater Cleveland area.